SOMEBODY FOREIGN

Douglas Post

BROADWAY PLAY PUBLISHING INC
224 E 62nd St, NY, NY 10065
www.broadwayplaypub.com
info@broadwayplaypub.com

SOMEBODY FOREIGN
© Copyright 2017 Douglas Post

All rights reserved. This work is fully protected under the copyright laws of the United States of America. No part of this publication may be photocopied, reproduced, stored in a retrieval system, or transmitted, in any form or by any means, electronic, mechanical, recording, or otherwise, without the prior permission of the publisher. Additional copies of this play are available from the publisher.

Written permission is required for live performance of any sort. This includes readings, cuttings, scenes, and excerpts. For amateur and stock performances, please contact Broadway Play Publishing Inc. For all other rights please contact Ron Gwiazda, Abrams Artists Agency, 275 Seventh Avenue, 26th Floor, NY, NY 10001, 646-461-9325.

Cover design by Don McLean

First edition: October 2017
I S B N: 978-0-88145-737-7

Book design: Marie Donovan
Page make-up: Adobe InDesign
Typeface: Palatino

SOMEBODY FOREIGN was developed in part through Prop Thtr Group's Midwest New Plays Festival and Stage Left Theatre's LeapFest New Work Festival, both in Chicago, Illinois.

SOMEBODY FOREIGN was first produced at City Lit Theater Company in Chicago, Illinois on 10 February 2006. The cast was as follows:

ROGER LEMONS	John Tomlinson
LIZ FLETCHER	Bethanny Alexander
BILL MOODY	Jim Schmid
AGENT CALDWELL	Greg Hardin
AGENT BATES	Charles W Glenn
ALAN FLETCHER	Shay Ames
PEGGY REED	Kelli Cousins
RUTH HICKEY	Niki Williams
GLORIA GILBERT	Kelli Cousins
ERIC BABCOCK	Shay Ames
FAITH ARMSTRONG	Niki Williams
DIRK SWANSON	Brian Plocharczyk
Director	Terry McCabe
Set design	Grant Sabin
Costume design	Ty Perry
Lighting design	Sean Mallary
Sound design	Terry McCabe
Production stage manager	Hazel Marie

CHARACTERS & SETTING

Roger Lemons, *an attorney, mid 30s*
Liz Fletcher, *an associate professor, early 30s*
Bill Moody, *a local chief of police, 50s*
Agent Caldwell, *an agent for the F B I, early 40s*
Agent Bates, *another agent for the F B I, late 20s*
Alan Sinclair, *Liz's brother, late 20s*
Peggy Reed, *Alan's fiancée, mid 20s*
Ruth Hickey, *Liz's friend, early 30s*
Gloria Gilbert, *a reporter*
Eric Babcock, *another reporter*
Faith Armstrong, *another reporter*
Dirk Swanson, *a car wash attendant, 20*

The roles of Peggy Reed *and* Gloria Gilbert *can be double-cast, as can the roles of* Alan Fletcher *and* Eric Babcock, *and* Ruth Hickey *and* Faith Armstrong. *In this way the play can be performed by a company of nine actors.*

Time: *The night of July 3rd.*

Place: *The conference room of a law firm in the city of Chicago.*

This play is dedicated to Terry McCabe,
Bethanny Alexander, and the first company of
SOMEBODY FOREIGN

"Justice is incidental to law and order."
J Edgar Hoover

Scene 1

(We are inside the conference room of a law firm in the city of Chicago. It is a modern space that has been meticulously planned out with a marble floor, floating window blinds and off-white walls, but it is also cold and somewhat sterile. There is a conference table and four chairs that speak of taste and money. At the moment we are looking at the residual effects of an extravagant office party. Champagne bottles and flutes line the floor. Red, white and blue confetti is scattered all across the room. It is night. ROGER *wanders through the aftermath of the festivities with a glass of bubbly in his hand.)*

ROGER: Usually we rent a penthouse suite. Or toddle down to Navy Pier where we mingle with the riff raff. But today, considering the circumstances, the fact that it's a red letter day, well… *(He looks around the room.)* A red, white and *blue* letter day, the *day* before the *day*, July the third, that is, not the fourth. You'd never get us near each other on an actual day off. And the fact that the firm is finally in this incredible new high-rise, this temple that we've built to ourselves, in the heart of the Loop. And… *(He attempts to dismiss it.)* The other thing… *(He continues.)* The partners wanted to celebrate. A big party. In a big room. The conference room. In our new surroundings. I'm with a law firm. I'm a lawyer. Don't hate me. *(He laughs.)* The fireworks are over and the others have gone home. To their wives and children and cherished possessions. That's probably where I should be. Instead I'm still here. Half drunk. Reeling from the heady news. The effects of the day. Lost in some… *(He shakes his head.)* I don't know what to call it. This feeling in my gut. The scraping sensation of a moral compass that spins one way. And then the other. *(He puts the flute down.)* And then I remember. Her.

(LIZ enters. She literally steps out of the shadows and goes to the front corner of the room. She is not actually in this room. Rather she is in the second floor hallway of a house somewhere outside of Chicago. She is holding herself. Clearly distressed. After a moment MOODY enters. He also steps out of the shadows and stands at a distance. Observing her)

LIZ: Oh, God.

MOODY: Um…Miss Fletcher?

LIZ: God.

MOODY: I'm sorry, I'm so…sorry, but I have to—

LIZ: Who would do something like this?

MOODY: I don't know. I honestly don't…I mean, I haven't seen anything like this since…I haven't seen anything like this. Ever.

LIZ: Why?

MOODY: I wish I knew. I wish I could offer some… reassurance or…idea of why this might have happened. I can't. It's beyond my… Look. We're going to find whoever did this. We will. And when we do, I promise you, that person will be hurt. And hurt badly. But right now I need your help.

LIZ: I don't understand.

MOODY: Neither do I. But it happened. And we have to…make an attempt. We do. Because I know who it is. Who they are. But I have to hear it from you. *(Pause)* Is that them? *(Pause)* Is that your brother and his fiancée lying dead in the next room?

LIZ: Yes.

(ROGER *continues to address the audience.*)

ROGER: Lake Sterling, Illinois. An upper-middle class college town on the outskirts of Chicago. One of those suburban enclaves where people move to get away from it all before realizing that *they* are *it*. And to them, to us, I should say, since I was there for most of it, the act itself was…incomprehensible. Alan Fletcher and his fiancée, Peggy Reed, had been found dead in the bedroom of their newly remodeled home. They had apparently been shot in their sleep with a four-fifty-four magnum. One right after the other. And Alan's sister, Liz Fletcher, had been brought to the scene of the crime so that she could identify the bodies. Peggy's family was downstate that weekend. In Springfield. And the police wanted to get their investigation going immediately. Liz gave them all the information she could. And then walked out of that house into absolute chaos.

(LIZ *turns to one side as the* COMPANY *now enters from all angles. They represent a collection of reporters and camera people who completely surround her.* MOODY *remains.*)

COMPANY: Excuse me, but can you tell us what's happened? We heard there was a killing. A double killing. Is that true? Is that accurate? Are you related to the deceased? Are you family? Is there anything you want to comment on? Anything at all? Please!

(*There is a blinding flash of light. All freeze.* ROGER *continues.*)

ROGER: Incomprehensible. Especially in this town with its stately mansions and well-manicured lawns. People were outraged. Incensed. But to some, to me, I suppose, since I was there for most of it, it wasn't so much the killings themselves that were so impossible to fathom as the events surrounding them. It started off some three months earlier. With a phone call.

(CALDWELL *emerges from the* COMPANY. MOODY *and the other members of the* COMPANY *exit.* CALDWELL *picks up a phone.* LIZ *picks up another phone.* ROGER *remains. The conceit of the play should now be clear. The story exists in* ROGER's *memory and as he tells it the confines of this room will come to represent a number of locations in the town of Lake Sterling and in the city of Chicago itself. There are no blackouts. One scene rolls right into the next.*)

Scene 2

ROGER: Liz was in her office that day at Lake Sterling University. A small but prestigious school with a national reputation for skeet shooting and tennis. The caller wouldn't identify himself to the receptionist. He would only say that he had to speak to Liz Fletcher. That it was a matter of life and death.

(LIZ *and* CALDWELL *are on opposite ends of a phone call. She is in her office going through some papers. He is elsewhere.*)

LIZ: Hello?

CALDWELL: Is this Liz Fletcher?

LIZ: Yes.

CALDWELL: My name is Agent Caldwell, ma'am. I'm with the F B I.

(Pause)

LIZ: I see. *(Pause)* What can I do for you, Mr Caldwell?

CALDWELL: I have to speak with you. Immediately. If not sooner.

LIZ: Why?

CALDWELL: Well, there's no easy way to say this.

LIZ: Say what?

CALDWELL: Are you sitting down?

LIZ: No, I'm standing. Speak. Please.

CALDWELL: Alright. *(Pause)* There's been a threat.

LIZ: A threat?

CALDWELL: Against your life.

LIZ: Really?

CALDWELL: Yes.

LIZ: By whom?

CALDWELL: What?

LIZ: Who threatened me?

CALDWELL: That's what I have to speak to you about.

LIZ: I'm listening.

CALDWELL: In person.

LIZ: Ah. *(Pause)* Well, I'm sorry, but I'm busy all morning.

CALDWELL: Then I'll come by this afternoon.

LIZ: No, I'm busy all day.

CALDWELL: Miss Fletcher, we have to talk.

LIZ: We're talking right now.

CALDWELL: Ma'am—

LIZ: Can you send me the information?

CALDWELL: I…what?

LIZ: Whatever information you have. Can you send it to me? In writing?

CALDWELL: I'm afraid I can't do that.

LIZ: Why not?

CALDWELL: Because it's confidential.

LIZ: What is? The information? Or the reason you can't send it to me?

CALDWELL: Well, actually, both.

LIZ: Right. *(Pause)* So this would be considered something of a federal secret.

CALDWELL: Well, I wouldn't—

LIZ: Should we meet in a parking garage?

CALDWELL: Sorry?

LIZ: Late at night? When no one's around?

CALDWELL: Uh—

LIZ: And you can answer to the name of Deep Throat? Or Long Dong? Or some other pornographic film star?

CALDWELL: Miss Fletcher, correct me if I'm wrong, but you don't seem to be taking this too seriously.

LIZ: Should I be?

CALDWELL: Look, I'm coming to see you first thing tomorrow morning.

LIZ: I teach a class.

CALDWELL: Then lunch.

LIZ: I work through.

CALDWELL: After work.

LIZ: I'll call you back.

(LIZ *hangs up. A moment.* CALDWELL *does the same.)*

ROGER: She didn't. And the following day Agent Caldwell came to her school. With his partner.

Scene 3

(BATES *enters. He and* CALDWELL *take their positions.* LIZ *walks towards them and almost past.* ROGER *remains. We are in a hallway in the university.*)

CALDWELL: Hello.

(She stops.)

LIZ: Who are you?

CALDWELL: We spoke yesterday morning on the phone.

LIZ: Mr Caldwell.

CALDWELL: Yes, ma'am.

LIZ: What are you doing here?

CALDWELL: You didn't call me back.

LIZ: I've been busy.

CALDWELL: This is Agent Bates.

BATES: How do you do?

LIZ: Well, I'd be doing a hell of a lot better if I knew how you men were able to locate me on campus.

BATES: I flashed the staff my winning smile.

CALDWELL: We spoke to your dean. He said you were on the third floor of this building. Teaching till two-fifteen.

BATES: Middle Eastern Studies. Hey, I read the course description. Sounds good. Slanted. But good.

CALDWELL: Look, Miss Fletcher, it's imperative that we talk.

LIZ: Not here.

CALDWELL: We have to speak to you about these threats.

LIZ: Not here!

CALDWELL: But—

LIZ: Not at my school!

CALDWELL: Ma'am—

LIZ: No! I would not come into your workplace, your situation of employment, and do something like this.

CALDWELL: We only wanted to—

LIZ: I will not talk to you!

CALDWELL: Then how are we to communicate?

LIZ: You make an appointment.

CALDWELL: What?

LIZ: You make an appointment like everybody else.

CALDWELL: You won't see me.

LIZ: I'll see you.

CALDWELL: You will?

LIZ: Yes. But not now. And not here.

CALDWELL: Then where?

LIZ: At your office. I'll come to your office.

BATES: You'll come and talk to us?

LIZ: What did I just say?

CALDWELL: When?

LIZ: Next Friday. Five o'clock. Is that good for you?

CALDWELL: Fine.

LIZ: You?

BATES: Hey, my time is your time.

LIZ: I'll see you then. *(She moves to another part of the room.)*

ROGER: And the following week Liz and I walked into the downtown offices of the Federal Bureau of Investigation.

Scene 4

(LIZ *turns.* ROGER *goes to her.* CALDWELL *and* BATES *turn to them. We are in an office of the F B I.)*

CALDWELL: Good afternoon, Miss Fletcher. You remember Agent Bates?

LIZ: How could I forget?

BATES: Who's he?

ROGER: I—

LIZ: This is Roger Lemons. I asked him to be here. As my attorney.

BATES: You brought a lawyer?

LIZ: Yes.

BATES: Why did you do that?

LIZ: I wanted to—

ROGER: Uh…Ms Fletcher thought it would be best to have someone else present when you disclose the nature of these threats.

LIZ: Alleged threats.

CALDWELL: There's nothing alleged about them.

BATES: So how do you feel about lawyer jokes?

ROGER: I happen to love them.

BATES: What do you call fifty lawyers buried up to their necks in cement?

LIZ: Not enough cement.

BATES: Well, now. You stole my punch line. Okay, a lawyer, a prostitute and a paid assassin walk into a bar.

CALDWELL: Uh, would anybody like some coffee?

LIZ: No.

ROGER: No, thanks.

CALDWELL: Donuts?

LIZ: Can we get started?

CALDWELL: Of course.

ROGER: My client and I are both anxious to hear about these...alleged threats.

CALDWELL: Well, they're against her.

ROGER: Yes.

CALDWELL: Against her life.

ROGER: Yes, I understand that, but whatever you have, whatever you've been able to ascertain, I'd like to see it.

CALDWELL: How do you mean?

ROGER: Well, don't you have something in writing?

CALDWELL: No.

ROGER: No?

CALDWELL: I'm afraid not. There's nothing on paper. Other than our notes.

ROGER: Isn't that unusual?

CALDWELL: Not especially. Our people in New York picked something up. We've got an informant in the Gaza Strip. A man who's been working in and around Hamas. And he's heard the same thing from a number of different sources.

ROGER: And that is?

CALDWELL: That there's been threats over there to kill Miss Fletcher if she ever again sets foot in the occupied territories.

ROGER: Why?

CALDWELL: Because she's suspected of being an informant.

LIZ: For who?

BATES: For us.

LIZ: For the F B I?

BATES: That's right.

LIZ: I'm suspected by Hamas of working for you?

CALDWELL: Correct.

LIZ: This is insane.

CALDWELL: Maybe. Maybe not. But we have to follow up.

ROGER: Yes, of course, I understand that, but—

LIZ: In what way?

CALDWELL: What?

LIZ: In what way do you intend to follow up?

CALDWELL: To do what we're doing. To warn you. And to ask you a few questions.

LIZ: Such as?

ROGER: Liz—

CALDWELL: You have traveled to the Middle East in the past, no? *(Pause)* Ma'am?

LIZ: Yes.

CALDWELL: Okay. Was it for business? Pleasure? *(Pause)* Miss Fletcher?

LIZ: I won't tell you that.

BATES: Look—

LIZ: No, there is no reason for you to know what I do there.

CALDWELL: Have you ever met anyone who you suspect might have a direct relationship with Hamas? Either their military operations? Or their money-raising efforts?

LIZ: Am I under investigation here?

CALDWELL: Of course not. We'd never even heard of you before this information landed at our feet. But we need to get some facts.

LIZ: Why?

CALDWELL: Well, that should be obvious.

LIZ: Enlighten me.

CALDWELL: So that we can protect you.

LIZ: From whom?

(CALDWELL *sighs.*)

BATES: This is going nowhere real fast.

CALDWELL: Miss Fletcher, have you had any dealings with people in the Chicago area who have expressed sympathy for Hamas and their stated aims?

ROGER: Uh, gentlemen, let me see if I understand this correctly. You're saying that my client has been threatened.

CALDWELL: Yes.

ROGER: Indirectly.

CALDWELL: That's correct.

ROGER: Why not directly?

BATES: What?

ROGER: Well, I mean, so far as I know, Ms Fletcher hasn't been personally accosted, right?

LIZ: That's right.

BATES: Maybe they want to surprise her. Catch her unawares.

CALDWELL: Sir, we're only trying to act on the information supplied to us by our informant. We don't have the full picture on how these people function. But we're trying to put the pieces together.

ROGER: Who is this man?

CALDWELL: Pardon me?

ROGER: This informant. Your man. What's his name?

CALDWELL: You know I can't tell you that.

ROGER: Why not?

BATES: Because it'd be like setting him up to be beaten senseless, kneecapped and knifed.

CALDWELL: And then killed.

BATES: Yeah, and then all that in reverse order.

ROGER: But he's talked to you.

CALDWELL: He's talked to our people.

BATES: And they talked to us.

CALDWELL: And I'm talking to you. That's the procedure. Now if we could please get back to these questions.

(LIZ *stands*.)

LIZ: No.

CALDWELL: I'm sorry?

LIZ: No, I won't answer your questions.

CALDWELL: Miss Fletcher—

LIZ: Not until you show me something in writing that proves these threats are real.

CALDWELL: Ma'am—

LIZ: Until then you are not to call me and you are not to come to my university.

ROGER: Uh, Liz—

LIZ: I'm sorry, Roger, but this conversation is over.

(LIZ *exits. A moment*)

ROGER: Well, as my client has decided to, uh…call the meeting to a close, I don't suppose there's any real point in my…being here. (*He stands.*) Gentlemen.

CALDWELL: Mr Lemons?

ROGER: Yes?

CALDWELL: Please tell her to be careful.

(*Pause*)

ROGER: I will.

Scene 5

(LIZ *enters carrying two drinks.* CALDWELL *and* BATES *exit.* LIZ *goes to* ROGER, *hands him a drink, and sits. He also sits. We are in a downtown bar.*)

LIZ: There is no threat.

ROGER: Liz—

LIZ: They made it up.

ROGER: How do you know?

LIZ: I *know* because that's the way they operate.

ROGER: The F B I?

LIZ: Look, it's no secret. They make life a living hell for anyone in this country even remotely connected with the Palestinian cause.

ROGER: But—

LIZ: Or they find out where you work and they come and harass you. Sometimes your employer doesn't like the fact that federal agents keep coming around on a regular basis. So you're fired.

ROGER: Yes, but—

LIZ: Or they follow you. Tap into your phone lines. Enter your house and do a sneak-and-peek. They're under no obligation to tell you now. Till months later when it's too late.

ROGER: Alright, but what does any of this have to do with you?

LIZ: Well, you know that I've been talking to my students about the political climate in the Middle East. Trying to get them to form their own opinions. Free from whatever bias they might have brought into the room.

ROGER: What else?

LIZ: I raise money for Amnesty International.

ROGER: What about these trips?

LIZ: What trips?

ROGER: The ones Agent Caldwell was asking about.

(Pause)

LIZ: I've been doing some research.

ROGER: For what?

LIZ: A book that I'm writing.

ROGER: Subject?

LIZ: The abuse of human rights in the Gaza Strip.

ROGER: Uh-huh.

LIZ: Don't be so smug.

ROGER: Liz, these are the people who refuse to recognize the right of Israel to even exist. Who want to see the whole state wiped right off the map. Who teach their children to become suicide bombers.

LIZ: What people are you talking about?

ROGER: The Palestinians.

LIZ: Yes, well, that's a beautiful, broad and sweeping generalization, Roger, but let me ask you something.

ROGER: Okay.

LIZ: How many Palestinians do you actually know?

ROGER: Do I know?

LIZ: How many have you met, sat down with, had a meal with?

ROGER: Well, I... *(Pause)* There's, um...okay, there's this... *(Pause)* Alright, point taken, but—

LIZ: The people I'm talking about are refugees. Living in camps. Their houses have been destroyed. Their water lines have been cut off. Their sewage systems are non-existent. Sixteen thousand men, women and children, my friend. Many of them pushed out of their homes for the second or third time.

ROGER: And why are their homes being destroyed in the first place?

LIZ: Because the Israeli Defense Force suspects them of building tunnels. Smuggling. Contraband.

ROGER: And arms. And explosives. And terrorists willing to use both.

LIZ: Ah, I was wondering when we'd get to the "T" word.

ROGER: Well, there it is.

LIZ: But the tunnels could be detected in other ways. They can be taken out without wreaking havoc. Even the U S uses sensors and radar along the border with Mexico. You don't see us tearing down houses. Turning people out into the desert.

ROGER: Alright, but—

LIZ: Even South Korea has a better plan for the D M Z.

ROGER: I'm sure they do.

LIZ: And the carnage is indiscriminate. It's not, "Look, let's take out this house over here because we think that's where the trouble's coming from." It's, "Let's level the whole damn block. Teach these bastards a lesson. Decimate them." And it does nothing. It only creates more mayhem. More catastrophe.

ROGER: I still don't understand what the F B I could hope to accomplish by telling you that someone was threatening your life.

LIZ: Names.

ROGER: I'm sorry?

LIZ: They want me to name names. To give them specifics on my contacts in the States. And probably in Gaza, too.

ROGER: Why?

LIZ: Well, look, you've seen how they work. Say that you were an activist.

ROGER: I'm not.

LIZ: A *human rights* activist.

ROGER: Okay.

LIZ: And I give them your name.

ROGER: Right.

LIZ: And they show up at your place of business and they say to you—

ROGER: They say, "What do you know about Liz Fletcher?"

LIZ: No, they say, "Liz Fletcher has been targeted by Hamas because they suspect that she's turned against them. That she's now giving information to us. What do you know about *that*?"

ROGER: And I would say, "Nothing."

LIZ: And they would go away.

ROGER: So what's been accomplished?

LIZ: You tell me.

ROGER: Well, I suppose I might…start to wonder.

LIZ: About what?

ROGER: Whether or not Liz Fletcher had ever worked for Hamas.

LIZ: Exactly.

ROGER: I don't know, Liz.

LIZ: What don't you know?

ROGER: Well, to begin with, they said they'd never even heard of you before this information came to them.

LIZ: And you believed them?

ROGER: Yes, I did. I *do*. And, what's more, why would they even be interested? What's in it for them? I mean, my God, we're talking about an agency that spent most of the sixties trying to decipher the lyrics to "Louie, Louie."

LIZ: Everything has changed since September Eleventh, Roger. The world's being reordered and reconfigured. And anyone who thinks to question, who asks if it's possible that we are doing more harm than good on this globe, is considered to be an enemy of the state.

ROGER: I hope you're not saying these things to your students.

LIZ: I'm very careful what I say to my students, thank you very much, but I also know what I feel. What I've learned from the past six summers in the Middle East. From listening to everything and discounting nothing. It all comes down to two states. Living side by side. Recognizing that one displaced people has displaced another. And acting responsibly. This is what needs to be done. What *has* to be done. But no one has the guts to do it.

ROGER: Well, you know what they say.

LIZ: What's that?

ROGER: Everything's negotiable.

LIZ: Right.

ROGER: Except for Israel.

LIZ: Except for Israel.

(LIZ *clinks her glass against* ROGER's *and drinks.*)

ROGER: So what do you want to do?

LIZ: What do you suggest?

ROGER: Give them some names.

LIZ: No.

ROGER: A few names.

LIZ: I won't.

ROGER: One name.

LIZ: I absolutely refuse.

ROGER: Why?

LIZ: Because for anyone I name, for anyone in Gaza or anywhere else who has taken me into their confidence, the results would be horrendous.

ROGER: You think that person's name would be passed along.

LIZ: I know it would.

ROGER: And that they'd be arrested.

LIZ: Yes.

ROGER: And go to prison.

LIZ: You can be held for six months now without being charged with anything.

ROGER: Alright, so you don't give them any names.

LIZ: What do I do?

ROGER: Ignore them.

LIZ: Yes?

ROGER: Go on about your business. Your...research.

LIZ: I will.

ROGER: And if they contact you again, you refer them directly to me.

LIZ: And you'll file charges.

ROGER: I'll...what?

LIZ: Charges of harassment.

ROGER: Maybe. Perhaps. I'll...do something. I promise. Alright?

LIZ: Alright. *(Pause)* Thank you, Roger.

ROGER: For what? Telling you what you wanted to hear? What you already knew?

LIZ: I didn't know if you'd return my call.

ROGER: Why?

LIZ: Didn't know if you were angry with me or—

ROGER: Why would I be angry with you?

LIZ: Well—

ROGER: I'm happily married, Liz. Really. Everything's worked out for the best.

LIZ: I miss talking to you.

ROGER: Well, now's your chance.

(LIZ *laughs. A moment.* LIZ *and* ROGER *look at each other.*)

ROGER: I'm sorry, I don't mean to be...flip.

LIZ: It's alright.

ROGER: It's good to see you. Really. You look...great.

LIZ: Thanks.

ROGER: So are you…seeing anyone or—?

LIZ: No. I mean, I've had a few dates recently, but most of the men I know seem…silly.

ROGER: Well, we are. We're a silly sex. That doesn't mean we're not capable of profound, emotional attachment. Between sporting events. And certain T V shows.

(LIZ *laughs again.*)

LIZ: You weren't like that.

ROGER: What was I like?

(Pause)

LIZ: I should go.

ROGER: Oh.

LIZ: No, really, I've got a kitchen table covered in papers.

ROGER: I remember that table.

LIZ: Look, I want you to bill me.

ROGER: No.

LIZ: I mean it.

ROGER: This one's on the house.

LIZ: No, I don't want charity. I can afford to pay for your services. And I intend to do so.

ROGER: Liz—

LIZ: Please don't fight me on this, Roger.

ROGER: Alright, alright, my firm will send you a bill, okay?

LIZ: Okay. *(Pause)* They're still working you too hard, aren't they?

ROGER: And paying me too little, but I want the partners to see that I'm meant for better things. Bigger cases. That I can roll with the punches.

LIZ: Well, don't be afraid to punch back, okay?

ROGER: Okay.

LIZ: Give my love to Miriam. *(She kisses him on the cheek.)* Goodnight.

(LIZ *exits.* ROGER *remains.)*

ROGER: I thought she was being more than a little paranoid. That she was spouting some party line fed to her by her friends in the human rights arena. And, no, I didn't share her outright distrust of everyone affiliated with the F B I. But I did want to know more about the basis of their inquiry. If, for no other reason, than to show her that she had nothing to be afraid of.

Scene 6

ROGER: Liz and I first met at a political fundraiser that I'd been pummeled into attending. I recognized her name. Her family name. Her father had been a respected business man who served on the board of Cook County. He twice ran for Congress. Twice lost. And finally retired to become something of an elder statesmen to his community. He'd passed away the previous summer. A stroke. Her mother died shortly after that. *(Pause)* I took to Liz immediately and, for a few months, we actually dated, before one of us, I think it was her, decided that we made better friends than lovers. *(He laughs.)* Alright, I *know* it was her. But she was right. I see that now. I wanted…more. From her. And, with Liz, the work always came first. Yes, I know, it's usually the other way around, but what can I tell you? I was smitten. A while later I met a woman who was more like me than not and, before I knew it, we were married. We invited Liz to the wedding, she came, but since then, well, I hadn't really been in touch. She'd called. Left a few messages. But then *this*. The F B I. I thought maybe I could actually be of some real use. And, at first, it seemed like I'd made the right decision in telling her to ignore the situation because, during the next three months, neither of us heard anything from Agents Caldwell or Bates. Her semester ended and summer break began. She flew overseas, continued her research, and returned several weeks later in high spirits.

(LIZ *enters with* ALAN *and* PEGGY. ROGER *exits.* ALAN *carries a glass of wine and a newspaper, which he tosses onto the table. He walks with a slight limp.* PEGGY *also carries a glass of wine and arranges the chairs around the table so that eventually they can all sit down. We are in their dining room.* LIZ *also carries a glass that she sips from as she takes in the room.)*

LIZ: Beautiful. It's beautiful. I can't believe the transformation.

ALAN: Thanks.

LIZ: The living room is fantastic. It's so open. And this dining room. The colors. Who picked them out?

ALAN: It was a mutual decision.

PEGGY: Alan bullied me into submission.

ALAN: Did not.

PEGGY: No, but I finally gave up. All those ridiculous names. "Misty Tangerine." "Adorable Peach."

LIZ: What did you finally go with?

PEGGY: I think it's called orange.

LIZ: Well, the house is done. That's the main thing.

PEGGY: Finally.

ALAN: I still have a list of small things to do, grouting the tub, installing hardware—

PEGGY: And the utility room's completely unfinished—

ALAN: But I'm giving myself a break.

PEGGY: Giving *us* a break.

ALAN: Yeah, Peggy tells me my disposition has been steadily deteriorating over the course of the last eighteen months, but that's what you get when you put your hard-earned money into "a handy man's dream."

PEGGY: What a euphemism. They should have said, "Total wreck in need of a torch." I almost moved back in with my old roommate just to give us a little breathing room, but I figured if we could get through this, we could get through anything.

ALAN: She was a first-class carpenter's helper.

PEGGY: I was sent out for a lot of beer.

LIZ: I never knew you were so handy.

ALAN: I'm not.

PEGGY: He's brilliant. He's read all the books now. He can do anything.

ALAN: Except work a nail gun.

PEGGY: Hey, it was your first time.

LIZ: Why? What happened?

PEGGY: Two weeks ago he was putting in the attic access—

ALAN: I'd been told that a power tool was the way to go.

PEGGY: I was down in the basement at the time taking cover. I called up. "Honey? Do you need help?" "No, no, I'm fine."

ALAN: Well, I thought I was okay.

PEGGY: He nailed his foot to the floor.

LIZ: What?

PEGGY: Nailed. His foot. To the floor.

LIZ: I noticed the limp, but—

PEGGY: With a sixteen-penny the size of my fist.

LIZ: Are you alright?

ALAN: Yes. Fine.

PEGGY: He took it like a man. Even tried to remove it himself. With a pair of rusty pliers.

ALAN: It was more humiliating than anything else.

LIZ: Let me see.

ALAN: No, Liz, really, I—

LIZ: Sit down and let me see.

PEGGY: Don't argue with her.

ALAN: Okay. *(He sits down and takes off his shoe.)*

PEGGY: We had to call an ambulance. Medics. Everyone at the hospital made a fuss.

ALAN: "Hey, look who's here! Al Fletcher! Class president. Rhodes scholar. Too bad you never took shop."

LIZ: So you got to relive your glory days.

ALAN: I got to eat an incredibly large piece of humble pie.

PEGGY: It's good for you.

(LIZ pulls her brother's leg up onto her lap and removes his sock.)

LIZ: Oh, my God.

(A huge bandage is wrapped around ALAN's foot.)

ALAN: It's not as bad as it looks.

LIZ: Did they clean this out?

ALAN: Yes.

LIZ: Stitches?

ALAN: I'm fine, Liz. Please, don't baby me. *(He takes back his leg and puts on his sock and shoe.)*

PEGGY: He doesn't like that.

LIZ: No, he doesn't. Never has. Even when he was in eighth grade and set his face on fire.

PEGGY: You never told me about this.

ALAN: You never asked.

LIZ: He was experimenting with a can of aerosol spray and a Bic lighter.

ALAN: Now that was painful.

LIZ: We had to tell Mom and Dad it was a bad case of acne.

PEGGY: They never found out?

ALAN: No.

LIZ: Oh, I think they knew.

ALAN: Not unless you told them.

LIZ: This is the first time I've mentioned it. *(Pause)* Today.

(They all laugh.)

LIZ: How are things at the day care center? Tell me everything. I want to know.

PEGGY: Good. The kids are great. I love them all. Even the toddlers with attitude. Little boys with mischief on their minds.

ALAN: It's good practice for dealing with me.

LIZ: Don't I know it. And Taylor Hawkins?

ALAN: I still like them. And they seem to like me. I never thought I'd end up like this, you know? A broker? Pontificating on the reduction of financial risk and diversification factors inherent in mutual funds?

PEGGY: With success.

ALAN: With some success.

LIZ: I always thought you'd go into politics.

ALAN: Well, who knows? Maybe I will. Someday.

PEGGY: Right after you find that cure for cancer.

ALAN: How was your trip?

LIZ: My trip. *(Pause)* Well, things are difficult right now. It's a difficult time. You can't even get into Gaza without signing a waiver.

ALAN: A waiver?

LIZ: Stating you accept that the Israeli government can't be held responsible for any damage or injury or death caused as a result of military activity.

PEGGY: Wait, this applies to you? To human rights workers?

LIZ: And peace activists. And foreign journalists. It's not a pretty scene. Not something the I D F wants reported in the international press. And none of this is helped, of course, by the fact that their Minister of Foreign Affairs has said that most human rights offices in the West Bank and Gaza Strip provide shelter for Palestinian terrorists.

ALAN: Which is not true.

LIZ: Which is absolutely not true. Still I was under constant scrutiny till I moved out. Stayed with a family in Rafah. A construction worker, his wife and two children. They made a place for me. A home. In this neighborhood where every house, every shelter, is shattered with bullet holes. We always made sure that one of us stayed inside because if the place is found empty, well, the D F will knock the structure down. We thought it was a good plan. A safe plan. Till one night, two A M or so, the military comes to call. They want us out. Now. We don't go. We hunker down. Prepared for the worst. Then it comes. They start shooting at the walls. The windows. *(Pause)* We had no choice. We got out. And the commander, this Israel kid barely out his teens, says, "Well, now the house is empty. Knock it down." So they do. With an armored bulldozer. And a ripper running after it that tears up the roads. The water. The sewage pipes. *(Pause)* I'm standing there. Shaking. The children are in tears. Their mother is screaming. Cursing. And this man, this incredibly decent man who took me in, says, "I spent thirteen years building homes for Israelis. I never thought the day would come when they'd destroy my house."

ALAN: God.

LIZ: And there's no future, really. No agriculture. The farms and gardens and greenhouses have all been demolished. The airport's damaged. The dock…well, there *is* no dock. No access. To anything. *(Pause)* And yet there I am. An American woman. With money. Employment. Security. Well… *(She laughs.)* Relative security.

ALAN: You're on a tenure track.

LIZ: Yes. A tenure track. A town home. My health. My little brother. His beautiful girlfriend. And these people have nothing. Next to nothing. And yet everyday they find a way to muddle through. And treat me with such kindness. Such unbelievable kindness. *(Pause)* Aren't you sorry you asked?

ALAN: No.

PEGGY: It's alright, Liz.

LIZ: No, it's not alright. Not before a meal. I promised myself, promised that I would not obsess this way.

PEGGY: It's okay.

LIZ: I'm so sorry.

PEGGY: We understand. We do. At least, I'd like to think we do. *(Pause)* No one can really, can they?

LIZ: No. Not unless you're there. Inside it. Even for myself, I find, the stories that I'm told, well, they only penetrate so far. Till I experience it. First hand. Or see a kid, a child, cowering in the street when… *(She stops herself. She shakes her head.)* I really think we should change the subject. *(She laughs.)*

PEGGY: Sure.

ALAN: Well, maybe this would be the time.

PEGGY: Maybe.

LIZ: What time?

ALAN: Here.

(ALAN *pushes the newspaper across the table to* LIZ.)

LIZ: *The Sterling Ledger.*

PEGGY: With all the local news.

ALAN: Plus bra ads.

LIZ: Well, I'm touched. Should I be looking at the classifieds? Do you know something I don't?

ALAN: Page twenty-three. The social listings.

LIZ: Did something happen while I was gone? *(She opens the paper. A moment. She smiles.)* This is a terrible picture. Of you, Alan. Total goofball. With bed hair. Peggy, you look lovely.

PEGGY: Thank you.

ALAN: It was spur of the moment.

PEGGY: We were painting the kitchen.

ALAN: I got down on my hands and knees.

PEGGY: He ran his brush around my finger. "Whimsical pink." Some of it's still there. *(She holds out her hand.)*

ALAN: It's a latex enamel semi-gloss.

LIZ: You couldn't afford the real thing?

ALAN: It's coming.

LIZ: Well.

ALAN: Are you mad?

LIZ: Are you kidding? I'm thrilled. My heart is racing.

*(*LIZ *stands and embraces both* ALAN *and* PEGGY.*)*

ALAN: We were going to wait till you got back, but—

LIZ: I don't care.

ALAN: Word got out.

LIZ: Obviously. When?

PEGGY: Next spring.

LIZ: Where?

PEGGY: The Methodist Church.

ALAN: Rick Hollinger's going to be my best man.

LIZ: Wasn't he your V P?

ALAN: Class secretary. Bill Esterhaus was my number two. He's catering.

PEGGY: And here's the thing, Liz. You know I don't have any sisters. Close girlfriends, yes, but— *(Pause)* I was hoping you'd be my maid of honor. *(Pause)* Lizzie?

LIZ: No, I was just thinking. *(Pause)* Dad would have loved being here. And Mom, too, of course, but especially Dad. He always loved our extended evenings together around a table. The stories we had to tell. The small accomplishments. He was always so proud. And he never forgot to say so. And now. Seeing you two today. With so much to be grateful for. To look forward to. Well, you know what he would have said.

ALAN: That we're blessed.

LIZ: Yes. Truly blessed. He'd have been so happy. *(To* PEGGY*)* I'd be honored.

Scene 7

*(*RUTH *enters carrying a violin case, sheet music and a music stand.* PEGGY *and* ALAN *exit.* LIZ *stands.* RUTH *puts down her paraphernalia. We are in the basement of the Lake Sterling Y M C A.)*

RUTH: Hello, stranger.

LIZ: Ruth! Hi! What are you doing here so early?

RUTH: It's my week to set up music stands.

*(*LIZ *and* RUTH *hug.)*

RUTH: What's your excuse?

LIZ: I thought I should get back in practice. With the Mendelssohn. And the Mozart. *(She picks up the sheet music.)*

RUTH: Everything okay?

LIZ: Yes. Fine.

RUTH: Good trip?

LIZ: Fine.

RUTH: Did you bring me anything?

*(*LIZ *laughs and produces a small package from her pocket.)*

LIZ: Earrings from Cairo.

RUTH: Not really.

LIZ: Really.

(RUTH *takes them out.*)

RUTH: Oh, I love them. I absolutely love them.

LIZ: Good.

RUTH: Thank you so much. (*She puts the earrings on.*)

LIZ: So what's been happening? What did I miss?

RUTH: Well, we're still complaining about the stench.

LIZ: The stench?

RUTH: The fact that this place always smells like a boy's locker room.

LIZ: Exactly how many times have you been in a boy's locker room?

RUTH: Once in college. Well, twice. I was dating a tight end.

(LIZ *laughs.*)

LIZ: So what did the staff say?

RUTH: About the aroma?

LIZ: Yes.

RUTH: Apparently there's a wrestling class right before us. And two sessions of aerobics right before them.

LIZ: We should move our rehearsal somewhere else.

RUTH: I know. I keep saying to Harriet, I say, "Honey, we are the Greater Chicagoland String Ensemble. What are we doing in the basement of the local Y M C A?"

LIZ: What does she say?

RUTH: "Playing badly."

LIZ: That is so unkind.

RUTH: Which is not to say that she hasn't gotten some bookings for us.

LIZ: Such as?

RUTH: A private party. Some corporate event.

LIZ: Please don't let it be Sears.

RUTH: Oh, that was such a fiasco.

LIZ: Everyone in the audience was completely soused. Hooting. Hollering.

RUTH: I know. To Samuel Barber.

LIZ: I refuse to go back.

RUTH: There might be a wedding.

LIZ: There will *definitely* be a wedding. We might even be asked to play.

RUTH: What do you know?

LIZ: Alan and Peggy are getting married!

RUTH: Really!

LIZ: It was in the paper.

RUTH: I can't read the paper. It depresses me.

LIZ: You can't read *The Ledger*?

RUTH: Am I in it?

LIZ: No.

RUTH: Then why bother?

(LIZ *laughs again.*)

LIZ: Well, anyway, it's been announced.

RUTH: That's great. That is just great. Not that I'm not all for shacking up, but it's like my mother used to say.

LIZ: Oh, no.

RUTH: "Why buy the cow if you can get the milk for free?"

LIZ: Your mother said this to you?

RUTH: Yes.

LIZ: And how did you feel about being compared to a barnyard animal?

RUTH: It didn't really bother me at the time, but now that I think back, it wasn't nice.

LIZ: No.

RUTH: So, then, I take it you haven't heard.

LIZ: Heard what?

RUTH: The really big news.

LIZ: What?

RUTH: Oh, nothing.

LIZ: Ruth!

RUTH: Other than the fact that the ensemble has been invited to perform overseas.

LIZ: No!

RUTH: To tour Europe.

LIZ: It's not true!

RUTH: It *is* true.

LIZ: But we're not any good.

RUTH: Yes, but the Europeans don't know that. And once we're there it'll be too late. They can't send us back.

LIZ: All of us?

RUTH: I know, it's ridiculous, but evidently Harriet has some connections and it's only for two weeks so, really, how much damage can we do?

LIZ: Where in Europe?

RUTH: France. Spain. Portugal. Or Poland. I'm not sure which.

LIZ: The continent! We'd be touring the continent!

RUTH: So you'll be able to go?

LIZ: Try and stop me.

RUTH: Oh, that's great. That's so great. Bob and I were hoping you could come. He plans on making a video of the entire event. You could room with us if you don't mind spending the second half of the trip watching the first.

LIZ: Oh—

RUTH: No, really, we could all bunk up together.

LIZ: Bunk up? *(She laughs.)* I don't think I've bunked up with anyone since we were in the Girl Scouts.

RUTH: I know, but it'd be fun. For me, if no one else. Say you will.

LIZ: Of course, I will.

RUTH: Thanks. Well. I'm going to get the rest of the stands. And my cello. Unless you need absolute silence in order to master your score.

LIZ: I'm still trying to figure out what key I'm in.

RUTH: Then I'll be right back. *(A moment)* It's good to see you, Liz.

LIZ: Good to see you, too, Ruth.

(RUTH *exits.* LIZ *sets up her sheet music. Then she removes her violin from its case. She sits and tunes her instrument. She is about to run the bow across a string when* RUTH *enters with* MOODY. *They both stand silently. Staring at* LIZ. *A moment. Then she turns. She looks at them.)*

MOODY: Miss Fletcher?

LIZ: Yes?

MOODY: I'm Chief Moody.

LIZ: Yes?

MOODY: Bill Moody with the Lake Sterling Police.

LIZ: What is it?

MOODY: I— *(Pause)* Can we step outside?

LIZ: Why?

MOODY: I need you to follow me in your car.

LIZ: Where? *(Pause)* What's happened?

(Pause)

MOODY: It's about your brother, Miss Fletcher.

Scene 8

(ROGER enters. LIZ, RUTH and MOODY exit.)

ROGER: One of Alan and Peggy's neighbors had become suspicious a few hours earlier when she noticed an open window at the side of the house. She walked over and saw a few small pieces of glass lying on the cement. The rest of the window was busted out and there was glass all over the basement floor. She'd phoned the police and they promptly arrived. They rang the bell, banged on the front door, and, finally, let themselves in. That's when they discovered the bodies. In the upstairs bedroom. Under the covers. A preliminary report revealed that nothing of any monetary value had been taken from the premises. The killer had left behind cash, credit cards and a state-of-the-art home entertainment system. He had apparently broken and entered for one reason only. To murder. Two innocent people.

(LIZ enters and goes to the front corner of the room. A moment. Then MOODY enters. He stands at a distance. We are once again in the hallway of PEGGY and ALAN's house. And we are back to the opening tableau of the play.)

LIZ: Oh, God.

MOODY: Um…Miss Fletcher?

LIZ: God.

MOODY: I'm sorry, I'm so…sorry, but I have to—

LIZ: Who would do something like this?

MOODY: I don't know. I honestly don't…I mean, I haven't seen anything like this since…I haven't seen anything like this. Ever.

LIZ: Why?

MOODY: I wish I knew. I wish I could offer some…reassurance or…idea of why this might have happened. I can't. It's beyond my… Look. We're going to find whoever did this. We will. And when we do, I promise you, that person will be hurt. And hurt badly. But right now I need your help.

LIZ: I don't understand.

MOODY: Neither do I. But it happened. And we have to…make an attempt. We do. Because I know who it is. Who they are. But I have to hear it from you. *(Pause)* Is that them? *(Pause)* Is that your brother and his fiancée lying dead in the next room?

LIZ: Yes.

(LIZ *turns. The* COMPANY *enters again from all angles as the collection of reporters and camera people who completely surround her.* MOODY *remains.*)

COMPANY: Excuse me, but can you tell us what's happened? We heard there was a killing. A double killing. Is that true? Is that accurate? Are you related to the deceased? Are you family? Is there anything you want to comment on? Anything at all? Please!

(*There is a blinding flash of light. All freeze.* ROGER *continues.*)

ROGER: That's the way I learned about it. Seeing Liz's face captured that way in a complete panic. On the ten o'clock news. I called her immediately. And when I didn't get any answer I went directly to her home.

Scene 9

(MOODY *and the other members of the* COMPANY *exit.* ROGER *turns to* LIZ. *We are in her home.*)

LIZ: Hello.

ROGER: Liz, I... *(Pause)* Have no idea what to say.

LIZ: What is there to say? I mean, really, what can be said?

ROGER: How are you doing?

LIZ: Not...well. I'm all...bent up inside. I can't seem to...focus.

ROGER: Oh, Liz.

LIZ: I mean, usually, when something like this happened...well, there's been nothing like this. Not even Dad's death. But when something occurred, I would call Alan. Or he'd call me. And that's how we'd get through it. That's how we'd manage. With each other.

ROGER: Have you been with people all day?

LIZ: Yes.

ROGER: The police?

LIZ: Yes, I've been with all of them, all day long, trying to think of anything I could possibly tell them that might be of some...use. Something they said to me. Something they did.

ROGER: You should have called me.

LIZ: I didn't want to talk to anyone.

ROGER: Do you want me to go?

LIZ: Yes. No. I don't...know. Stay if you like. Yes, stay for a minute.

ROGER: Okay.

LIZ: Oh, my God, Roger. Who would want to hurt them? The two of them?

ROGER: The police have—

LIZ: No idea. None. It could have been anyone.

ROGER: I'm so sorry, Liz.

LIZ: Yes.

ROGER: I really am so sorry.

LIZ: I mean, I was with him. Last night. And Peggy was there. And she was so…happy. So… *(Pause)* They were *there*. I was *talking* to them. Telling them about my travels. And they listened. Intently. The way they always do. While I babble on. About people they've never met. Never even heard of. In some distant surroundings. But, of course, I knew what he was thinking. My brother. That I was the senseless one. Me, with my causes that keep me in perpetual motion. Because for him, life is so simple. Everybody loves him. He's got no enemies. None. Only friends who would do anything for him. He walks into a room and people light up. He changes the atmosphere. With his smile. His manner. *(Pause)* And then this morning. To see him that way. His face. His body. Covered in…blood. And then to watch them take him away. And all the while I'm thinking… *(Pause)* I'm thinking to myself… *(Pause)* I will never, ever…see my baby brother…again.

(LIZ *breaks down.* ROGER *goes to her. He holds her. She sobs uncontrollably. Nothing is said between them. He holds her tight. She buries her face in his chest. Then she disengages herself and exits.*)

Scene 10

ROGER: The funeral was two days later. I was there. With a lot of people from Liz's university. Her string ensemble. Her community, I think. It's hard to say. My memory of that particular occasion is like something from a dream. The ceremony, the faces, the words that were said, it was all so...unspeakably sad. *(Pause)* I didn't talk to Liz again for about a week. Then she called me. She'd heard from Agent Caldwell. He wanted her to meet him at the Lake Sterling Police Station. And she wanted me to be there.

(MOODY enters with CALDWELL and BATES. ROGER turns to them. We are in the Lake Sterling Police Station.)

MOODY: Mr Lemons?

ROGER: Yes.

MOODY: I'm Bill Moody.

ROGER: Yes.

MOODY: These are Agents Caldwell and Bates.

ROGER: We've met.

MOODY: Well. Miss Fletcher isn't here yet. Would you like to sit down?

ROGER: Sure.

(ROGER does. Then MOODY sits. CALDWELL and BATES remain standing.)

MOODY: Do you live around here, Mr Lemons?

ROGER: Do I?

MOODY: Yes.

ROGER: No. I...my wife and I live in the city.

MOODY: Kids?

ROGER: Uh...not yet.

MOODY: One of life's blessings.

ROGER: So they say.

(Silence)

BATES: Anybody hear how the game went?

MOODY: Cubs lost.

BATES: They did?

MOODY: Yes, sir.

BATES: By a lot?

MOODY: See, that I don't know. I only heard that they lost.

BATES: Huh.

(*Silence*)

MOODY: So let me ask you boys something. This Hoover. J Edgar?

CALDWELL: Yeah?

MOODY: Was he funny or what?

BATES: Funny?

MOODY: The boy-toy. The cross-dressing. I mean, what do you think?

(*Pause*)

CALDWELL: We try not to live in the past.

(LIZ *enters.* MOODY *stands.*)

LIZ: I'm sorry I'm late.

MOODY: Miss Fletcher.

LIZ: Hello, Chief.

MOODY: These are—

LIZ: Yes, I know. Thank you for coming, Roger.

ROGER: Of course.

CALDWELL: We were extremely sorry to hear about your brother and his fiancée, Miss Fletcher.

LIZ: Thank you.

BATES: We sent flowers.

LIZ: I'm sure somebody got them.

MOODY: How are you, ma'am?

LIZ: How am I? *(Pause)* I can't sleep. Can't eat. Can't hold down food. I've got these blotches on my arms. I don't know where they came from. I took a bath this morning for the first time in several days. I barely recognized myself in the mirror. I feel mostly as if I have been hit by a truck and knocked onto another continent. That's how I am. *(Pause)* What is this about?

CALDWELL: We think there's a connection here.

LIZ: Between?

CALDWELL: Between the death threats we intercepted last spring.

LIZ: And what?

CALDWELL: The killing of your brother.

(Pause)

LIZ: You…you think—?

BATES: We think that Hamas intended to kill you and got him and his fiancée by mistake.

LIZ: That's ridiculous.

ROGER: I have to say, gentlemen, it's a real stretch.

LIZ: It's fiction.

CALDWELL: It is certainly not fiction, Miss Fletcher. It's a conclusion that we reached based upon the evidence we've received.

LIZ: Has it occurred to you that they have never murdered a single person on American soil? That they confine their attacks to Israel? And the occupied territories?

BATES: There's always a first time.

LIZ: That they publicly take credit for each and every one of their killings?

BATES: Maybe that's still to come.

LIZ: And that it would have been a hell of a lot easier to kill me two weeks ago when I was in Gaza?

CALDWELL: Look, Miss Fletcher—

LIZ: No, you look. At me. Do I appear to be anything like Peggy Reed? Would you mistake me for her? *(To* BATES*)* Would you? *(To* MOODY*)* Would you?

MOODY: Well, I—

CALDWELL: The fact is you're not listed.

LIZ: What?

CALDWELL: In the phone book.

(Pause)

BATES: Any reason for that?

LIZ: I like my privacy.

BATES: Everybody does.

CALDWELL: So they come here to Lake Sterling looking for a Fletcher. They find your brother's address. They go to his house.

BATES: And they break in.

CALDWELL: It's dark. They don't turn on the lights. They make their way upstairs. Quietly. And they find a couple asleep in bed.

BATES: Maybe they think you're married. That he's your husband. And…it happens.

LIZ: Do you honestly think that Hamas would send someone into the center of the Midwest to assassinate a small-time human rights activist?

CALDWELL: What *rights* would you be referring to, Miss Fletcher? *(Pause)* You said you were in Gaza two weeks ago? Why? *(Pause)* Who do you know inside this terrorist organization?

ROGER: Liz, as your attorney, I advise you not to answer these questions.

LIZ: I don't intend to.

CALDWELL: You're not going to help us?

LIZ: There is nothing...there is no connection here. My brother and his fiancée were brutally murdered. In their home. By someone—

BATES: Who?

LIZ: I don't *know* who! That's what the police are supposed to be figuring out. Not listening to this fabrication without a single fact to back it up.

CALDWELL: We have our facts.

LIZ: Show me.

CALDWELL: Our sources.

LIZ: You have scare tactics and that's all.

MOODY: Look, Miss Fletcher, I know that you're upset, but I have to seriously consider any leads that come my way.

LIZ: This is not a lead. It's an outright lie.

MOODY: We don't know that.

LIZ: Jesus Christ.

CALDWELL: So you refuse to provide us with any information.

LIZ: I do.

CALDWELL: Fine. Come on, Bates. *(He starts to go.)*

BATES: You know, Miss Fletcher, if I didn't know better, I'd say you weren't interested in finding the person who murdered your brother and his bride-to-be.

(Pause)

LIZ: Goddamn you.

ROGER: Liz—

LIZ: Goddamn you and take you straight to hell, you son-of-a-bitch bureaucrat.

BATES: Well, now you've really cut me to the quick, haven't you?

CALDWELL: Bates—

BATES: You've called me a couple of bad names.

CALDWELL: Let's go.

BATES: But we'll be talking to you again. And when we do it'll be with your full cooperation. Count on it.

(CALDWELL *and* BATES *exit.*)

MOODY: You have to understand, Miss Fletcher. These men came to me. I have a responsibility to listen to them.

ROGER: Chief?

MOODY: Yes?

ROGER: Would you excuse us?

MOODY: Of course.

(Pause. Nobody moves.)

ROGER: Would you mind leaving the room?

MOODY: Well, I— *(Pause)* Sure. *(He exits.)*

ROGER: Liz, we have to talk.

LIZ: Bastards.

ROGER: Yes, they're bastards, and we have to talk.

LIZ: About what?

ROGER: The fact that you need to get yourself a lawyer.

LIZ: I have a lawyer.

ROGER: A criminal lawyer.

LIZ: You've practiced criminal law.

ROGER: We both know my bread and butter is commercial litigation, contractual disputes—

LIZ: So study up.

ROGER: Liz—

LIZ: No. I want you to represent me, Roger. Whatever happens. I don't want to bring in somebody from the outside. Not now.

ROGER: But there are better people, more experienced people, than—

LIZ: Than you, yes, I'm sure of it. Lawyers with endless credentials. Attorneys who could talk rings around these agents. But I trust you! *(Pause)* I trust *you*. *(Pause)* Am I wrong to do so?

ROGER: No. No, of course not. But, please, please, listen to me—

LIZ: No. You listen. To me. You've seen these people up close. You know what they're capable of.

ROGER: And?

LIZ: And you heard one of them threaten me.

ROGER: So?

LIZ: So file a Freedom of Information Act and see what the F B I actually has on this alleged death threat.

ROGER: I already have.

(Pause)

LIZ: You—?

ROGER: I did it already.

LIZ: When?

ROGER: Three months ago.

(Pause)

LIZ: After you told me to ignore them?

ROGER: Yes.

LIZ: And?

ROGER: It finally came through this morning. *(Pause)* They've been collecting information on you for seven years, Liz. *(Pause)* Seven years. *(Pause)* Did you hear what I said?

LIZ: Yes.

ROGER: And you remember—?

LIZ: That they said they'd never heard of me before this information landed at their feet. Yes, I remember that. And I remember that you believed them.

ROGER: Yes, I— *(Pause)* I did. *(He goes to the window and looks out.)* What do you want me to do?

LIZ: Promise me.

ROGER: What?

LIZ: That whatever happens you'll remain my legal counsel.

(Pause)

ROGER: Alright.

LIZ: And my friend.

(Pause)

ROGER: I'll always be here for you. I promise.

(A moment. LIZ goes to ROGER. She lingers.)

LIZ: I made a big mistake in letting you go, didn't I?

ROGER: Big. Mistake.

(LIZ smiles.)

LIZ: Oh, well.

(She turns and exits. ROGER *remains alone in the room. A moment)*

ROGER: The next day we were the top story on the ten o'clock news.

Scene 11

*(*ROGER *picks up a T V remote control, points it at us and presses a button as* GLORIA *enters and addresses the audience.)*

GLORIA: In Lake Sterling today police announced that the main lead they are pursuing in the murder case of Alan Fletcher and Peggy Reed extends far beyond the relative tranquility of this small town. Three months ago, Alan's sister, Liz Fletcher, an Associate Professor of Middle Eastern Studies at Lake Sterling University, was told that the F B I had received several threats against her life. Apparently the terrorist organization known as Hamas decided that Fletcher had turned against them, even though, as an activist, she has worked on behalf of Palestinians in the Gaza Strip. Ms Fletcher ignored these threats at the time. But now sources say that Hamas may have actually sent someone to Lake Sterling. Someone who mistook Fletcher's fiancée for Liz Fletcher herself. And brutally ended the lives of Peggy Reed and the man she would marry. Gloria Gilbert. Channel Two News.

ROGER: And two days later.

*(*ROGER *presses the remote again as* ERIC *enters and does the same.)*

ERIC: Local authorities in Lake Sterling are now saying that they are considering two separate theories regarding the recent murders of Alan Fletcher and Peggy Reed. One theory has it that Hamas thought Ms Reed was actually Liz Fletcher, a woman who has championed the plight of the Palestinian people, but who, in recent months, has apparently fallen into disfavor with this terrorist sect. The other theory is that the couple, who were engaged to be married, were killed as a warning to Fletcher's older sister. Ms Fletcher herself has refused to comment on the case other than to say that she rejects any theory linking this tragedy to Hamas and that to do so, she believes, is an attempt by federal authorities to undermine both her efforts and a legitimate human rights movement. Eric Babcock. Channel Seven News.

ROGER: And the following day.

(ROGER *presses the remote again as* FAITH *enters and does the same.*)

FAITH: Police today say they are following a number of different leads in an attempt to solve the bloody murders of Alan Fletcher and Peggy Reed. Among these are business dealings, financial affairs and interpersonal relationships. But the prominent theory, and the one that continues to haunt this community, is the Middle East connection. Were Fletcher and his fiancée the innocent victims of an act of international terrorism? Only Liz Fletcher knows. And she's not talking. Faith Armstrong. Channel Five News.

(MOODY *enters and* ERIC *turns to him as* ROGER *presses the remote again.*)

ERIC: We're speaking with Lake Sterling Police Chief Bill Moody. Chief Moody, are there any new leads in your investigation of the double murders?

MOODY: Leads. We always have leads. I'll tell you this. My job would be a heck of a lot easier if I could talk to Liz Fletcher and find out what she knows.

ERIC: Ms Fletcher is still refusing to cooperate with the police?

MOODY: Yes, she is.

ERIC: And what do you make of this?

MOODY: Well, if it were *my* brother, I'd want to know who did it. And I would do everything within my power to assist the local authorities. Period.

(ROGER *presses the remote again as* FAITH *speaks.*)

FAITH: Another angle the police are pursuing on the Lake Sterling murders is the possibility that terrorists had wanted to kidnap Alan Fletcher and use him as a bargaining tool against his activist sister, Liz Fletcher.

(ROGER *puts down the remote and goes to* ERIC.)

ERIC: I'm with Roger Lemons, the spokesman and attorney for Liz Fletcher. Mr Lemons, will Ms Fletcher now come forward and talk to the police?

ROGER: Ms Fletcher is only too willing to help the police in their efforts. What she is *not* willing to do is assist the F B I in a witch hunt designed to root out information about her contacts in the human rights community.

ERIC: Are you saying that your client has something to hide?

ROGER: I'm saying that she is not about to dignify a line of inquiry that has no basis in reality. She will, however, discuss any other theories the police want to talk about.

ERIC: With an attorney present?

ROGER: With an attorney present.

GLORIA: Chief Moody, do you have any comment in response to Mr Lemons's statement?

MOODY: Well, I'm happy to know that Liz Fletcher is willing to cooperate with our investigation, but why does she need a lawyer with her in order to do so? I mean, if I were innocent, I'd come in and put all my cards out on the table. And I think most people around here would do the same.

GLORIA: And you still believe that these killings may have international repercussions?

MOODY: I believe it is entirely possible that these crimes were committed by somebody, or *somebodies*, foreign to this soil.

GLORIA: The question remains: What does Liz Fletcher know and when will she share that information with the people investigating her brother's death? Back to you, Steve.

Scene 12

(ROGER *goes to a phone and dials.* MOODY, GLORIA, ERIC, *and* FAITH *exit. The other phone rings.* LIZ *enters and answers it. She is in her home.* ROGER *is elsewhere.*)

LIZ: Hello?

ROGER: It's me.

(Pause. She slides to the floor.)

How are you doing?

LIZ: Alright, considering. I feel besieged.

ROGER: That's because you *are* besieged.

LIZ: Today at the train station. All those newspapers. And my name in the headlines. I tried to act normal. But I can't.

ROGER: No.

LIZ: Even ordinary conversation takes on a hidden meaning.

ROGER: How are things at work?

LIZ: Well, they would be a hell of a lot better if the press would stop using the name of the university in every story they write about me. My dean's a tolerant man, but the trustees are beginning to talk.

ROGER: Can you go somewhere?

LIZ: What do you mean?

ROGER: Take some time off? A trip? Out of town?

LIZ: I'm going to Europe this fall with my ensemble.

ROGER: Before then.

LIZ: No, I've got too many commitments.

ROGER: Of course.

LIZ: Can't we do something?

ROGER: I don't know what else to do.

LIZ: I mean, they make me sound like a criminal!

ROGER: Do you want to talk?

LIZ: To who?

ROGER: The police?

LIZ: And say what? What else is there to say? I've told them everything I know!

ROGER: Then there's nothing we can do.

(Pause)

LIZ: Are you suggesting that I should?

ROGER: What?

LIZ: Sit down with them?

ROGER: Are you seriously interested in my opinion?

LIZ: Why else would I ask?

ROGER: Then I would say, yes. Yes, whatever information you have. Turn it over.

(LIZ *sits up.*)

LIZ: What?

ROGER: Look, I know this isn't what you want to hear, but there are things that are more important to me at this moment than your sense of idealism.

LIZ: Like what?

ROGER: Your safety. Your sanity. *(Pause)* If the people you know, if the ones you've been interviewing overseas, really are innocent of all wrong doing, then they should have nothing to be afraid of. Alright, the authorities might come to them. Ask them some questions. Even take them into custody. But if they're innocent, the truth will eventually come out. They'll be released. This is Israel, Liz. This is our ally. They don't hold civilians without cause. They don't kill for no good reason. And if there's any chance, even the slightest possibility, that the people you're in contact with are guilty, or can get to the ones who are guilty, the ones perpetuating these senseless attacks, this holy war, well, then, yes, they should be incarcerated.

LIZ: Roger, you don't—

ROGER: You asked me what I thought, so I'm telling you. I hate saying this. Hate what's happening to you. But you can make it all go away, Liz. It's in your power. *(Pause)* Think about it, okay? *(Pause)* Okay?

LIZ: Alright.

(Pause)

ROGER: Now can I ask you something?

LIZ: What?

ROGER: How the hell did a nice girl like you get mixed up with all these crazy Arab nationalists?

*(*LIZ *laughs.)*

LIZ: Oh, I don't know. Too much time spent reading *The Arabian Nights*, I suppose. You know, *Ali Baba and the Forty Thieves*.

ROGER: Seriously.

LIZ: Seriously? *(Pause)* When I was girl we traveled abroad. My father could afford it and he thought it was a good thing for the family. To be exposed to life outside this country. We took a cruise through the Mediterranean Sea and went to Greece, Cyprus and then on into the Holy Land, because he thought we should see that, as well. Mom and Dad fought about it, I remember, but in the end he won out.

ROGER: Uh-huh.

LIZ: Well, we saw everything. The Basilica, the Dome of the Rock, the Western Wall. That's where I met her. This beautiful Arab-Israeli girl with big brown eyes and a gold tooth. Sticking pieces of paper. Into the cracks. *(Pause)* I asked her what she was doing and she said that she was helping her father. He worked at the Postal Authority's center for undeliverable mail. And some of the stuff they got, well, they were letters. From all around the world. Addressed to God. No one knew why they ended up in Jerusalem, but they did. People asking for good health. For work. To be released from debt. From a relationship. *(She laughs.)* One man wanted forgiveness for stealing money from a grocery store as a child. So she took it upon herself, this girl, to see that the letters went into the wall. That these people's prayers found their proper destination.

ROGER: What was her name?

LIZ: Maritza Nazif. She was two months older than me and we took to each other immediately. Her English was excellent. Better than mine. And she thought it was thrilling to meet an American girl. She wanted to know all about the States, our music, our television.

She came to the hotel where my family was staying. We had lunch together. Took a walk. Talked for hours. Then another day I met her family. Two little brothers, her mother and father. And her cat. Abu. Then it was time for us to go home. I told her I'd write when I got back. To her, not God. And I did.

ROGER: You became pen pals.

LIZ: Yes. I used to send her a letter once a month and she'd respond almost immediately. We kept the correspondence going for two or three years. Then several months went by and I didn't hear from her. Finally, a letter came. She was sorry she hadn't written sooner and then she proceeded to explain why. Her family had gone to see her aunt in Ramallah. Her mother was pregnant at the time and on the way back she went into early labor. Their car was in a line at the checkpoint to get back into Israel, to a hospital, when this happened, but there was some problem with their papers and the guards wouldn't let them through. Her mother was bleeding, the baby was coming, but there was no reasoning with anyone.

ROGER: Don't tell me.

LIZ: Maritza's little sister was stillborn. Her mom survived. But her father, well, he went out of his mind. He picked up a tire iron and went after one of the guards, but before he could even land his first blow, he was shot. Killed on the spot. By gunmen in a tower. *(Pause)* Maritza, her brothers and her mother went back to Ramallah. To be with her aunt. To live.

ROGER: Jesus.

LIZ: I tried to write back, but I couldn't. I didn't know what to say. There was nothing in my life that I could compare it to. I could only think, it could have been me. My family. My dad.

ROGER: And Maritza?

LIZ: What?

ROGER: Did you ever…see her again?

LIZ: No. *(Pause)* No, I never did. *(Pause)* Roger?

ROGER: Yes?

LIZ: Who do you think did it?

ROGER: Did what?

LIZ: Who do you think killed my brother?

ROGER: I— *(Pause)* Don't know.

LIZ: Do you think we'll ever know?

ROGER: Yes.

LIZ: How?

ROGER: They'll find the person.

LIZ: Yes, but how? When everybody's convinced it was an international incident? A terrorist attack? How will we find out? How will we know?

ROGER: I can't say. I only know that…these things have a way of surfacing.

LIZ: By themselves?

ROGER: Sometimes.

LIZ: Well, I wish I had *your* sense of idealism. *(Pause)* I should let you go.

ROGER: Alright. *(Pause)* I'll call you tomorrow.

LIZ: Okay.

(LIZ hangs up. A moment. Then ROGER does the same and exits. She stays on the floor. RUTH enters and dials the phone. The other phone rings. LIZ answers it.)

LIZ: Hello?

RUTH: Liz?

LIZ: Yes?

RUTH: It's Ruth.

LIZ: Hi.

RUTH: I need to see you.

LIZ: What's wrong?

RUTH: I need to talk to you.

LIZ: What's the matter, Ruth?

RUTH: Oh, God.

LIZ: Where are you? (*She stands.*)

RUTH: Home.

LIZ: I'll be right over.

RUTH: No! (*Pause*) No, they might be watching.

LIZ: They?

RUTH: Meet me at the IHOP.

LIZ: Ruth?

RUTH: The IHOP! In ten minutes! Meet me there!

(RUTH *hangs up. A moment. Then* LIZ *hangs up and exits.*)

Scene 13

(RUTH *crosses to the table and sits. A moment. Then* LIZ *enters. She sees* RUTH. *She crosses and sits opposite her. We are in a restaurant known as the International House of Pancakes.*)

LIZ: I would love to know what's going on.

RUTH: They came to the house.

LIZ: Who?

RUTH: Some men.

LIZ: The press?

RUTH: No.

LIZ: Police?

RUTH: Federal.

(Pause)

LIZ: Federal agents came to your home?

RUTH: Yes.

LIZ: Why?

RUTH: They wanted to talk about you.

(Pause)

LIZ: About me.

RUTH: Bob had taken the kids to soccer practice. I didn't know what to do.

LIZ: What did they want to know, Ruth?

RUTH: Everything. *(Pause)* They said they thought you might have gotten friendly with someone.

LIZ: Friendly?

RUTH: That you'd dated someone. The wrong someone. And that you'd talked to this person about Hamas. And that Hamas found out about it. And they were angry. So they sent a man to Lake Sterling. *(Pause)* They wanted to know who you see. Who you don't see. What sort of men you like. What *you're* like. Politically. Socially. Sexually.

LIZ: God.

RUTH: They said, if I was really your friend, I would help them.

LIZ: And did you?

(Pause)

RUTH: Liz, do you remember all those emails you sent me?

LIZ: Yes.

RUTH: The ones from the Middle East?

LIZ: Oh, Ruth.

RUTH: What?

LIZ: You didn't—?

RUTH: Didn't what?

LIZ: You didn't give them those emails?

RUTH: No, no. Of course not. I never even printed them out.

LIZ: Good.

(Pause)

RUTH: I gave them my computer.

LIZ: You what?

RUTH: My laptop. I don't know why. They asked. And I did. And I felt terrible for doing it.

LIZ: But you did it anyway.

RUTH: Are you angry?

LIZ: Yes.

RUTH: Liz, I was terrified.

LIZ: Why?

RUTH: Because of what happened to Alan and Peggy.

LIZ: But that's not going to happen to you.

RUTH: How do you know that? How can you be so sure? Maybe you said something to them.

LIZ: What would I say?

RUTH: Something that got them killed. And, and, whoever killed them might think that you said something to me. That I might know something.

LIZ: What would you know?

RUTH: I don't know anything!

LIZ: Who put these ideas in your head? *(Pause)* They did, didn't they?

RUTH: Liz, if you would only talk to the police.

LIZ: No.

RUTH: The F B I.

LIZ: I can't.

RUTH: If you would just cooperate!

LIZ: Cooperate. *(Pause)* They told you to tell me that, didn't they? *(Pause)* They asked you to ask me.

(Pause)

RUTH: Yes.

(LIZ *gets up from the table.*)

RUTH: Liz!

LIZ: I think I'll skip the pancakes. *(She exits.)*

Scene 14

(CALDWELL *enters carrying a file.* RUTH *exits. A moment. Then* LIZ *enters. We are in an office of the F B I.*)

CALDWELL: Miss Fletcher.

LIZ: I know what you're doing.

CALDWELL: How did you get past the front desk?

LIZ: I flashed them your partner's winning smile. Right now I'm all teeth. I'm aware of the fact that you're talking to my friends.

CALDWELL: Oh?

LIZ: You went to see Ruth Hickey.

CALDWELL: I did?

LIZ: And Dotty Burke.

CALDWELL: Uh-huh. Anybody else?

LIZ: Stan Talbert. Tom and Betty Reistroffer. The Brewsters. The Cohens. And most of the members of my string ensemble.

CALDWELL: And why would I be doing this?

LIZ: Because you're attempting to turn them against me. Because you think I'll somehow crack under the pressure. Which I won't.

CALDWELL: No, I can see that.

LIZ: You people have put a roving wiretap on me.

CALDWELL: Really?

LIZ: My work phone. My home phone. My cell phone.

CALDWELL: Uh-huh.

LIZ: That's how you got to them.

CALDWELL: Anything else?

LIZ: I have reason to believe that you've been inside my house.

CALDWELL: Doing what exactly?

LIZ: Going through my records. My research.

CALDWELL: Thanks, but I think I'll wait for the book to come out.

LIZ: How do you know I'm writing a book?

(Pause)

CALDWELL: Isn't that what all academics do?

LIZ: Not all.

CALDWELL: Well, then, I was misinformed. *(Pause)* And why would we...I'm sorry. *I. I* seem to be personally responsible for all of the problems in your life. Why would I be doing all this?

LIZ: To get the facts. To intimidate my friends. My colleagues.

CALDWELL: Into doing what?

LIZ: Giving you information on me.

CALDWELL: On you?

LIZ: Yes.

CALDWELL: You have an overblown sense of self-importance, Miss Fletcher. Has anyone ever told you that?

LIZ: I want that laptop back.

CALDWELL: What laptop?

LIZ: The one you took from Ruth Hickey.

CALDWELL: I have no idea what you're talking about.

LIZ: You have no right.

CALDWELL: No?

LIZ: No subpoena.

CALDWELL: You want me to get a subpoena? You want to go to court? Because I can pick up the phone and do it faster than you can change your mind.

LIZ: Give me that computer!

CALDWELL: Can I say something as a personal observation?

LIZ: No.

CALDWELL: You're paranoid.

LIZ: Paranoid?

CALDWELL: I assume that you know the clinical definition of the word.

LIZ: You have decimated my life! You have broken every law you purport to uphold! You are a sickness!

CALDWELL: Sickness? Do you really want to see a sickness? *(He throws the file that he is carrying down on the table.)* Guess what hit my desk this morning? The report on Mordecai University in Tel Aviv. Ever heard of it?

LIZ: Of course.

CALDWELL: Well, you're going to be hearing a lot more. A suicide bomber walked into the cafeteria earlier today and blew himself up. He took ten faculty with him. And seventeen students. Want to see?

LIZ: I'd rather—

(CALDWELL flips open the file and pushes a series of photographs out onto the table.)

CALDWELL: Fifty-nine other people are in the hospital, Miss Fletcher, and the folks you're talking to over there have taken complete responsibility.

LIZ: I don't know anyone in the militant wing of Hamas!

CALDWELL: Are you kidding me? Do you think these people walk around with their Hamas militant wing membership cards hanging out? There is overt and there is covert. And they are all over the map. Raising money. Recruiting. And killing anyone who gets in their way including Palestinians they deem disloyal to the cause. *(Pause)* Please, do me a favor, because despite what you might think, I really don't like seeing people in pain, and that includes you. Talk to the police. *(Pause)* Talk to the police, Miss Fletcher. Tell them what you know. What you don't know. Tell them what you surmise. Tell. Them. Everything.

(LIZ looks at the photos. She looks at CALDWELL. A moment.)

LIZ: Alright. *(Pause)* Alright, I'll do it. *(Pause)* I'll talk to the police.

Scene 15

(ROGER *enters.* CALDWELL *exits. We are in the Lake Sterling Police Station.*)

ROGER: I'm so glad that you're doing this, Liz.

LIZ: Yes, I know.

ROGER: I mean, whatever your decision was, wherever you arrived, I would respect it. But I really do think that this is the right course. For everyone involved.

LIZ: I hope so.

ROGER: So what are you going to say?

LIZ: Anything that might be of help.

ROGER: Such as?

(MOODY *enters.*)

MOODY: Miss Fletcher, how are you doing? I have to say, I was glad, I was awfully glad, to hear from you. Relieved, is the word. Go ahead, sit down. Sit, sit.

(*They do.*)

MOODY: The truth is this situation hasn't been easy on any of us. We wanted, needed your cooperation from the start. And somehow, I don't know what happened. Goddamn Federal people come in and everything gets turned around. But now it's just you and me. And, ah...

ROGER: Lemons.

MOODY: Mr Lemons. Of course. So. (*Pause*) So what do you have to tell me?

LIZ: I've been thinking about that night.

MOODY: What night?

LIZ: The night he was killed. *They* were killed. I'd been at their home. For dinner. I told you this.

MOODY: Yes.

LIZ: And I told you how Peggy had told me about Alan hurting himself. With the nail gun. While he was putting in the attic access and she was downstairs in the basement.

MOODY: Okay.

LIZ: And right before it happened she called to him.

MOODY: She said—

LIZ: "Honey? Do you need help?" And he called back, "No, no, I'm fine."

MOODY: I remember. You were trying to be helpful. Telling me everything they'd said the previous evening.

LIZ: So now think.

MOODY: I am.

LIZ: Nothing?

(MOODY *sighs*.)

MOODY: Miss Fletcher—

LIZ: You've been saying they were upstairs, on the second floor, when the basement window was broken.

MOODY: They were.

LIZ: Then why didn't they hear it? *(Pause)* Why didn't they hear the window breaking and get out of bed? Why didn't they come downstairs? At least meet the killer halfway? If Alan could hear Peggy calling him from the basement, don't you think he would have heard that? Reacted to that?

MOODY: He was sleeping. They both were.

LIZ: Maybe. *(Pause)* And then there's the window itself. The glass. You told me that most of it was in the basement, but there was a smattering of it left outside.

MOODY: On the cement. Yes.

LIZ: Why would that happen?

MOODY: I don't really pretend to understand the nature of glass, Miss Fletcher, but—

LIZ: I do. I ran an experiment. Busted out my basement window.

ROGER: You—?

LIZ: Yes?

(Pause)

ROGER: You broke a window?

LIZ: Two of them. In my town house.

ROGER: I see.

LIZ: From inside.

MOODY: Why?

LIZ: To see what would happen to the glass. It all went out. Out onto the patio. Nothing fell inside. Nothing remained. But when I went outside and picked most of it up and threw it back into my basement, guess what?

MOODY: There was something left.

LIZ: A smattering.

(Pause)

MOODY: Are you suggesting that the glass was broken from inside?

LIZ: No. I'm telling you. That's what happened.

MOODY: Then how did the killer get into the house?

LIZ: He was let in.

ROGER: What?

LIZ: He was let into the house. For whatever reason. Maybe it was someone they knew. Someone they recognized. And after it was over he smashed the window. To make it look like something else. Like he had broken and entered.

MOODY: I don't think so.

LIZ: No?

MOODY: No.

LIZ: Well, considering that every other theory you've constructed comes straight out of a graphic novel, I'd give it a moment's thought.

MOODY: What is this about?

LIZ: It's about the fact that you have chosen to ignore every piece of evidence that's fallen down in front of you in favor of something flashier, something sexier, and something certain to make the ten o'clock news.

MOODY: Miss Fletcher—

LIZ: Why aren't you doing what a policeman should be doing instead of courting the media?

MOODY: Ma'am—

LIZ: Why aren't you out policing?

(MOODY *stands.*)

MOODY: I will not have you come in here and tell me my job!

LIZ: Well, obviously, somebody has to.

ROGER: Okay, Liz—

MOODY: Get out of here! Get out of my office!

LIZ: I thought you wanted my help.

ROGER: We should go now.

MOODY: I don't need your help! I'll find the person who did this crime! Without you! And when I do, I can promise you one thing, Miss Fletcher. It, it'll be—

LIZ: Star material?

MOODY: Get out!

(LIZ *and* ROGER *exit.* MOODY *sits. A moment. Then* BATES *enters.*)

BATES: Well?

MOODY: Well what?

BATES: I didn't hear anything that sounded like a full disclosure.

(ROGER *enters.*)

ROGER: I'm sorry, but I left my— *(He sees* BATES.*)* Pen.

(A moment. BATES *and* ROGER *stare at each other.)*

ROGER: I thought this was a private conversation.

BATES: Hey, I just walked in.

ROGER: Uh-huh. *(He picks up his pen and starts to go.)*

BATES: "What have we done to bring this on ourselves?"

(ROGER *stops.*)

ROGER: Sorry?

BATES: That's what the Dalai Lama said. When Tibet was invaded by China. "What have we done to bring this on ourselves?"

(ROGER *moves toward* BATES.)

ROGER: Are you suggesting that Ms Fletcher is somehow responsible for her own misfortunes?

BATES: "What have we done to bring this on ourselves?"

(BATES *turns and goes. Then* MOODY *goes. Then* ROGER *pockets the pen.*)

Scene 16

ROGER: During the next few months Alan and Peggy's killer remained at large and the name of Liz Fletcher continued to haunt the headlines. Then it was late fall and Liz got ready to go to Europe with the other members of her ensemble. She was exhausted by this time. Physically and emotionally drained. And ready to get on a plane and go somewhere else.

(LIZ *enters and sits.* ROGER *exits. A moment. Then* RUTH *enters. We are at O'Hare International Airport.*)

RUTH: Liz?

LIZ: Hello, Ruth.

RUTH: Can I sit?

LIZ: Of course.

(RUTH *does.*)

RUTH: God, I never thought I'd get through security. They took my scissors, my nail clippers, even my eyebrow pencil. Now how is that supposed to be used for a weapon? Can you tell me? Could anyone possibly take down a plane with a pointy crayon? Honestly. I don't know where I am anymore, but as soon as we land, I need to find a Walgreens. Or whatever it is they have over there. *(Pause)* You know, I've never been out of the country before. Can you believe it? Well, once. We went to Cancun. But that hardly qualifies. *(Pause)* Do you want some gum?

LIZ: No.

RUTH: Everyone is so excited. Especially Bob. He's loaded down with maps and guide books. Of course, he's got every day planned out. Really. To the last second. I said, "Bob, maybe we could go somewhere else besides Euro Disney." He said, "It's there. We should see it." *(Pause)* I got the laptop.

LIZ: The what?

RUTH: The laptop they took from me. They sent it back. I guess they decided they didn't need it. Or they copied the hard drive. I don't know. *(Pause)* I am so deeply sorry, Liz.

LIZ: It's alright, Ruth.

RUTH: I can't tell you.

LIZ: No, it really is alright.

RUTH: I feel so ashamed.

LIZ: Don't. You were pressured into it. By people who had no right to be talking to you in the first place. It doesn't matter now. It really doesn't. All that matters is that you and I and the Greater Chicagoland String Ensemble will be getting out of this country for awhile. God, what a relief.

RUTH: Yes. *(Pause)* Look, I know this is probably the worst possible time to be bringing this up.

LIZ: What's that?

RUTH: It's only that some of the others, some people in the bus on the way out, well, they wanted me to say something because, because after all—

LIZ: Ruth, what is it?

RUTH: You and I are friends.

LIZ: What?

RUTH: Aren't we?

LIZ: Yes, of course. *(Pause)* Tell me.

RUTH: Well, there's a feeling, a general sense, that maybe, maybe with the flight and all, and things being the way they are, you know, the international situation—

LIZ: You think that I should room with someone else. *(She laughs. A moment)* You think I should take another flight. *(Pause)* You think I should stay here.

RUTH: It's not my idea, Liz.

LIZ: No.

RUTH: It's only that, that—

LIZ: No, of course, you're right. All of you. It's much better if I stay behind.

RUTH: For you, too.

LIZ: Yes, of course, for me. Well, thank you. Thank you all for being so selflessly concerned with my well-being.

RUTH: We only wanted to—

LIZ: Because, I mean, after all, when it comes right down to it, I could be running guns for the Islamic Resistance Movement.

RUTH: Oh, God, Liz, you're not, are you?

(LIZ only stares at RUTH. A moment. Then RUTH exits.)

Scene 17

(LIZ finds a bottle of wine. She picks up an imaginary pebble. And she throws it into imaginary water. ROGER enters. We are on a beach.)

ROGER: Good afternoon.

LIZ: Hi, there.

(ROGER stands watching LIZ for a moment.)

ROGER: I got your message. I'm sorry I couldn't make it by earlier, but the, uh…partners brought me in on a discussion.

LIZ: It's alright.

ROGER: Anyway, I got out of there as soon as I could. I went to your home, but there was no answer. Then someone, some neighbor, said you'd decided to drive down to the beach. *(Pause)* How are you doing?

LIZ: Five seems to be my limit.

ROGER: Five?

LIZ: Skips. Well, four and a half, actually. I can't seem to find any flat, round stones.

(Pause)

ROGER: I heard about the trip.

LIZ: Oh? From who?

ROGER: It was in the paper. I'm sorry about that, Liz. I know you were looking forward to it.

LIZ: Yes, I was. *(Pause)* I got fired today.

ROGER: What?

LIZ: Released from my responsibilities.

ROGER: How?

LIZ: Quickly. I was told to clear out my desk. My office. My T As are taking over my classes. Twenty-two-year-olds who can't complete a single thought without using the word "whatever."

ROGER: The school can't do that.

LIZ: Oh, yes, they can.

ROGER: Why?

LIZ: Because they don't like me anymore. No, that's not true. They seem to like me fine. They just don't like the publicity I'm bringing to their sacred campus. It creates the wrong image. The wrong effect.

ROGER: They can't fire you for that.

LIZ: No, of course, they can't. They told me that they're letting me go because my work has been less than stellar. Because my students have been complaining about incompetence.

ROGER: And have you been?

LIZ: What?

ROGER: Incompetent?

(LIZ *turns and stares at* ROGER. *A moment*)

ROGER: No, I guess not.

LIZ: It's got nothing to do with my performance, Roger. It's got everything to do with the *fucking* F B I and the police and the media.

ROGER: So sue.

(LIZ *laughs.*)

LIZ: Yes, well, that would surely take my name right out of the headlines, now wouldn't it?

ROGER: Do it anyway.

LIZ: No, please. I don't want a fight. I really don't. I just want…I don't know what I want. No, I do, actually. I want to surrender.

ROGER: Liz—

LIZ: Almost. *(Pause)* I mean, I would, I really would walk away from it all if I didn't have your help. Your support. *(Pause)* I still have it, right? *(Pause)* Roger?

ROGER: The firm wants to take me onto the next level.

LIZ: That's wonderful.

ROGER: What that means specifically, I don't know, but I suspect that they're talking about bigger clients, larger lawsuits. There's this case of tortious interference that—

LIZ: A partnership?

ROGER: That word hasn't been broached.

LIZ: But they must be thinking about it if—

ROGER: Yes, I mean, I suppose it's a possibility, but here's the thing. *(Pause)* They've indicated— *(Pause)* The suggestion has been made that it would be a better use of my time if—

(Pause)

LIZ: You have to say it.

ROGER: They want me to drop the case.

(A moment. Then LIZ turns away.)

ROGER: It's not what you think, Liz. These are decent people I work for. I mean, the politics of the situation was never even mentioned.

LIZ: Of course not.

ROGER: But with the new responsibilities they say that my time will be somewhat limited.

LIZ: It's okay, Roger.

ROGER: And the fact is that you haven't exactly been overly interested in my opinions from the start.

LIZ: No, that's true.

ROGER: I mean, I'll stay with you if that's what you want. I'll explain to them that I've made a commitment here. They'll understand.

LIZ: Isn't there a salary increase?

ROGER: Yes, of course, but—

LIZ: Then you should take it. Take the increase and build Miriam a home in the Western suburbs. Go on vacation. Have a family. You deserve it. You've done enough for me. More than I had a right to expect.

ROGER: Liz, if—

LIZ: No, it's decided. It is. Let's not talk about it anymore.

(Pause)

ROGER: What will you do?

LIZ: I don't know. I really don't. Throw another stone. *(She does.)*

ROGER: I counted six.

LIZ: Well, there it is. My new calling. *(Pause)* My father. My father used to say the nice thing about living in a small town is that you get to know your neighbors. He was right.

(LIZ goes to ROGER. She gives him a full embrace as if to forgive him and to say goodbye. Slowly, awkwardly, his arms go up around her. A moment. Then she pulls away and starts to go. She is almost off. Then she turns and looks back at him.)

LIZ: Do you know what I think?

ROGER: About what?

LIZ: When they catch him?

ROGER: Who? *(Pause)* Oh.

LIZ: I think it'll turn out to be someone anonymous. Someone you'd pass on the street and think nothing about. Someone who bags groceries. Or cuts hair. Or collects income tax.

ROGER: Maybe. *(Pause)* Or maybe you were right the first time.

LIZ: When?

ROGER: Maybe we'll never know.

(Pause)

LIZ: Goodnight, Roger.

(LIZ exits. A moment. ROGER stands looking out at the water.)

Scene 18

ROGER: Two months later the owner of a local car wash walked into the Lake Sterling Police Station and told the sergeant at the desk that he thought one of his employees, Dirk Swanson, might be responsible for the murders of Alan Fletcher and Peggy Reed. Evidently Swanson, a twenty-year-old high school dropout and social misfit, had been threatening to pistol-whip someone at work. He mentioned a weapon. A Freedom Arms four-fifty-four. The police went to his home with a warrant, found the handgun, and arrested him. The bullets in the gun matched the bullets recovered from the scene of the crime. Swanson made a full confession.

(DIRK *enters and addresses the audience.*)

DIRK: It was a Friday night. There was nothing going on. I'd just been with this girl, this Mary Beth Brackenridge, who'd given me a real hard time about wanting to get into her pants. I left her house and went out walking. There was a party happening over at Conroy's, but I didn't want to go there. I sat in the parking lot at the liquor store for a while and watched the idiots go in and out. I asked some loser to buy me a six-pack of Mickey's Big Mouth and he said no. Then I remembered the gun. I'd got it off this freak that said his sister had lent it to him. I went back to the house, my house, and the old man was watching some shit about America's most wanted. I got the piece and left. *(Pause)* I went looking for a house, a big place with all the lights turned on. With people inside. Then I found it. Nice lawn. Nice lawn furniture. A bird-feeder. Wind chimes. The works. I looked in the window and saw this guy with two women. One of them was on her way out. I watched her get in her car and go. Then I made my move. I went right up to the front door and rang the bell. Ballsy, I know. The guy answered and I told him I was collecting for the Boy's Club. I love that part, because in Lake Sterling, see, there is no Boy's Club. He could have saved himself a world of trouble if he'd known that simple fact. He let me in. He got his wallet. And that's when I pulled out the gun. I told him to sit down. The woman walked into the room and I told her to sit, too. They tried to talk to me, to figure me out or some shit, and I said, "Shut up." *(Pause)* The furniture inside was nice, too. All new. Everything smelled like fresh paint. And their faces. They were cute. A cute couple. Wholesome. I turned off the lights and we sat there. For an hour. Maybe two. Then I told them I was tired and wanted to go home. That they should go upstairs and get ready for bed. I said, if they did what I wanted they wouldn't get hurt. They went up. I followed them. They got undressed. Put on their matching t-shirts and sleep pants. I think that's when I decided. I made them lie down on the mattress. I made them cover up. Then I fired the gun into him and into her. *(Pause)* It was time to go now, but I wanted to be smart about it. I went downstairs into the basement and found some gloves. Work gloves. And a hammer. I wailed on the window. Bam! The glass went out. I unlocked the window and pushed it up. I left through the back door and locked it behind me. I looked at the window and the broken glass lying on the cement. It didn't look right to me. I picked up all the big chunks and tossed them back inside. I walked away. Whistling. Then I went home. *(Pause)* People want to know why I did it. My friends. Family. The police. I'm not sure. Some days I think I know and then I don't. But it seems to me those two people had it coming. They were irritating. *(A moment. Then he exits.)*

ROGER: Swanson had a history of bad behavior that included beating up an ex-girlfriend, bludgeoning a security guard with a golf club, and firing a handgun into the ceiling of a church. He had been charged with domestic battery, aggravated battery and unlawful use of a weapon. In all three cases, he'd been found guilty, fined, put on probation, required to take anger management classes, and medication. Swanson spent his Saturday mornings washing cars at the Lake Sterling Police Station. He was there the morning after the murders. In fact, he was there every Saturday morning until he was finally turned in. No one had ever interviewed him. No one had even talked to him.

Scene 19

(GLORIA *enters.* ROGER *remains.*)

GLORIA: Dirk Swanson was found guilty today of the murders of Alan Fletcher and Peggy Reed. Inside sources say they expect him to receive two consecutive sentences of life in prison without parole.

(MOODY *enters and* GLORIA *turns to him.*)

GLORIA: Chief Moody, do you have any thoughts at this late date regarding how this investigation might have been handled differently?

MOODY: Well, sure, there's always hindsight. But, hey, look, we found the killer. And that's what counts.

GLORIA: And as for all of the attention focused on Liz Fletcher?

MOODY: That came to us. The F B I opened the door and we went in. Sure, I feel badly. But this was a case of murder. And when you're dealing with something that big, well, people are going to get hurt.

GLORIA: When asked what role they had in the misdirection of this case, the F B I offered no comment.

MOODY: And, let me just say, that the media blew this whole thing—

GLORIA: Gloria Gilbert. Channel Two News.

(GLORIA *and* MOODY *exit.*)

ROGER: And that's the way it ended. For most of us. We simply flipped to another channel and found another story. *(He finds a bottle of champagne. He fills his flute. He looks at it.)* I should go home. We're expecting, you see. Twins in August. And I've already raised several glasses to the holiday. And the high-rise facility. Oh, and for myself, I forgot to mention. *(He raises his glass.)* Today they made me a full partner. Cheers. *(And he downs the entire drink.)* I think about her a lot. Her stubbornness. Her tenacity. And that first day. When her life was turned upside down.

(LIZ *enters and goes to the front corner of the room. A moment. Then* MOODY *turns to her. He stands at a distance. We are back to the opening tableau of the play.*)

MOODY: Is that them? *(Pause)* Is that your brother and his fiancée lying dead in the next room?

LIZ: Yes.

(LIZ *turns. The* COMPANY *enters again as the collection of reporters and camera people who completely surround her.* MOODY *remains.*)

COMPANY: Excuse me, but can you tell us what's happened? We heard there was a killing. A double killing. Is that true? Is that accurate? Are you related to the deceased? Are you family? Is there anything you want to comment on? Anything at all? Please!

(There is a blinding flash of light. All freeze. ROGER *continues.)*

ROGER: Liz Fletcher left Lake Sterling that fall. In fact, she left the country. She moved to Gaza City and went to work at the Palestinian Center for Human Rights. I wrote her. Often. At first she wrote back every week. Then every month. Then every three months. Then I got a Christmas card. *(Pause)* Then I stopped hearing from her altogether.

(ROGER *remains motionless in the room. Night. Silence.)*

END OF PLAY